Mind Magnet

Harness the Invisible Power of Thought to Attract the Life You Desire

By

Jonathan W. Hale

Copyright 2025

All rights reserved

Chapter 1: **The Magnetic Power of Thought**

Our universe operates under one vast and unified principle—**Law**. Although it expresses itself in countless ways, behind all its manifestations lies a single foundational force. We're familiar with some of these expressions, like gravity or motion, yet many others remain elusive or poorly understood. However, with each passing day, more of this cosmic truth is revealed, slowly lifting the veil that has long obscured the full picture.

We speak confidently about the Law of Gravity and other well-established physical principles, but we often overlook one of the most powerful forces that influences our lives: **the Law of Attraction as it operates in the realm of thought**. Just as gravity binds us to Earth and holds planets in their orbits, there exists an equally potent, invisible force that draws experiences, people, and outcomes toward us based on the nature of our thinking.

Most people accept the idea that physical matter is held together by invisible bonds—atomic attractions, gravitational pulls, and electromagnetic fields. Yet those same individuals tend to dismiss the equally valid idea that **our thoughts**, too, exert a magnetic pull, drawing circumstances into our lives that mirror our internal mental states. We give scientific names to physical laws, but the energetic force of thought—its pull, its echo—is rarely discussed with the same seriousness.

The moment we start seeing **thought as a form of energy**, a real and active force vibrating on its own frequency, we open the door to understanding many things that previously seemed mysterious or out of reach. Realizing this truth transforms how we see our lives and empowers us to live with intention rather than by default.

Among all subjects available for study and personal mastery, **none offers a greater return** than understanding how the Law of Attraction functions in the thought world. It is both subtle and immense—an invisible engine running beneath the surface of all that we do, shaping our experiences, relationships, and future outcomes.

When you think, you emit **vibrations of an extremely fine and high-frequency energy**. These vibrations are just as real as those that create sound, light, heat, or electricity. The fact that these mental energies cannot be detected by our standard five senses does not invalidate their existence. A lack of perception is not proof of nonexistence.

Consider a powerful magnet: it exerts an unseen force strong enough to lift heavy metal objects. You can't taste, hear, or see this force, but you can measure its effects. Thought vibrations work in a similar way—they are invisible, but they carry real influence. Some highly sensitive individuals can even detect these thought-waves directly, often described in cases of telepathy or emotional intuition.

In fact, many of us have experienced moments where we've **felt another person's thoughts**, whether we were physically near them or not. You might walk into a room and instantly feel tension or joy—this is not your imagination, but a response to real energetic signals emitted by those present. These are subtle but undeniable interactions between minds.

What some people dismiss as "vibes" are actually **waves of thought energy**, silently communicating beyond words. Phenomena like telepathy and intuitive perception may seem fringe to some, but they are rooted in the same laws that govern the movement of other energies. Science, while still catching up in terms of measurement tools, is gradually recognizing this truth.

Interestingly, waves of light and heat exist on **vibrational spectrums lower** than that of thought. The difference lies only in frequency, not in reality. Modern physics continues to explore these invisible ranges, stretching our understanding of what can exist beyond our senses. As science pushes its boundaries, it continually uncovers forms of motion and frequency that were previously deemed impossible.

For instance, Professor Elisha Gray, in his work *The Miracles of Nature*, once reflected on the possibility of **undetectable sound-waves and invisible color-vibrations**, suggesting that between the known ranges of sound and light exists an entire unexplored realm of motion. He wasn't claiming proof—he was pointing toward possibility, inviting speculation and curiosity.

Similarly, M. M. Williams, in his book *Short Chapters in Science*, described the vast vibrational gap between sound and heat, implying the likely presence of **an undiscovered world of energy**. According to him, this energetic domain could very well produce sensations—experiences—if only we had the proper instruments or biological receptors to perceive them.

I share these ideas not to prove anything through authority, but to offer you a broader framework for contemplation. Those who have truly explored thought energy already know that its presence is **more than theoretical**—it's deeply experiential and verifiable through self-observation. If you pause and reflect, you'll likely see examples of this law at play in your own life.

We've all heard the expression, "Thoughts are things." It's said often, sometimes even casually, but do we truly understand what that means? If we did—if we grasped the **literal, energetic reality of our thoughts**—we would realize how immense their impact is. Our thoughts aren't just ideas floating around in our heads; they are **forces**, capable of shaping the very structure of our lives.

Every time you think, you activate a high-frequency wave that moves out into the world. Understanding how those waves operate—how they're generated, how they move, and what they interact with—enables you to work with them intentionally, just as we've learned to harness electricity or sound waves. Just because we cannot weigh or photograph a thought doesn't mean it isn't real.

For example, many sound waves go beyond human hearing, though they may still be picked up by insects or machines. The same applies to thought vibrations—many of which remain undetected by our current tools but are still exerting influence. Instruments are slowly evolving to sense subtler energies, and **in the future**, we may have devices that detect thought patterns just as we now record sound and light.

Even if such tools don't yet exist, the human mind itself is already the most advanced mechanism for receiving and sending these vibrations. Those who practice **telepathy, visualization, and focused intention** have experienced this directly. And for them, no further scientific validation is necessary—they know from personal experience.

Whether you realize it or not, you are **constantly broadcasting mental signals**, and the world is responding. Your thoughts not only influence your personal state—they influence others and attract circumstances, people, and events that resonate with them. If your thoughts are rooted in love, confidence, and clarity, that's what you'll begin to see more of. If your thoughts dwell in fear, anger, or doubt, you'll attract experiences that confirm those patterns.

For instance, a mind filled with love will draw in affection, kindness, and emotional harmony. On the other hand, if you constantly think thoughts of resentment or criticism, you will attract people and circumstances that echo those same emotions. **Like attracts like**—in thoughts just as in nature.

Hold a certain type of thought persistently, and you'll become **a magnet** for matching energy from others. This law doesn't care if you're aware of it or not—it simply responds to the **vibrational frequency** of your mind. It operates consistently and impartially.

This is why someone who wakes up in a bad mood can end up experiencing a cascade of negativity throughout the day. A person who constantly nags usually finds more reasons to complain. Conversely, someone who radiates calm and assurance can walk through chaos untouched, like a ship gliding smoothly through a storm. Their inner energy becomes the oil that quiets the waves around them.

The Law of Attraction is not just a curiosity—it's a **fundamental truth** that shapes your entire reality. Once you grasp this, you'll start to take full responsibility for the energy you emit and the life you create. You'll stop blaming others and start noticing how your internal world mirrors back through your experiences.

There are people who've mastered this. They've learned to hold steady, clear, empowering thoughts even while surrounded by conflict or negativity. These individuals don't merely survive the storms of life—they influence their environment by the strength of their inner state. They radiate mental stability that acts like an anchor in the winds of chaos.

We've already lived through the age of physical dominance, then moved into the era of intellectual achievement. Now, humanity is stepping into a new frontier: **the age of energetic and mental mastery**. This new domain is governed by its own laws, and those who learn to understand and apply them will shape the future—not through force or intellect alone, but through **intention and vibration**.

The time has come to study this inner science. Like electricity or steam, the power of thought can be used constructively once understood. It can heal, uplift, attract, and transform. You are the operator of the most powerful instrument in existence—your mind.

And now, you're going to learn how to use it.

Chapter 2: **Thought Waves and the Frequencies of Mental Resonance**

Imagine dropping a pebble into still water. It sends ripples outward in perfect circles. Thoughts work the same way—but on a much more powerful level. The difference is that while water ripples travel across a flat surface, **thought waves radiate in all directions**—not just outward on a horizontal plane, but in every dimension, like rays from the sun.

Just as Earth is surrounded by an atmosphere of air, we are immersed in a vast, invisible sea of mental energy. Our thoughts don't simply bounce around inside our heads—they move outward into this mental ether, sending vibrations in all directions. These waves may weaken slightly as they travel farther, due to the natural resistance of the mental environment, but **they keep moving nonetheless**, affecting everything they pass through.

Thought waves are more than just echoes in the mind—they carry a unique quality: **the ability to reproduce themselves**. In this way, they are more like sound waves than ripples on water. When you play a note on a violin near a thin wine glass, the glass may begin to vibrate sympathetically, even "sing," in harmony with the note. In the same way, **a strong thought can awaken matching vibrations in the minds of others** who are tuned to the same mental frequency.

Many of the random thoughts that pop into your mind are not necessarily yours. They may be **echoes or reflections**—responses to powerful thoughts sent out by someone else, received by you because your mental state was aligned to pick them up. If your mind is consistently focused on high, positive, or creative thoughts, your "mental tuner" becomes attuned to that range. You begin to naturally receive similar vibrations from others operating at the same level.

But the reverse is also true. If you get into a pattern of thinking negative, petty, or fearful thoughts, your mental frequency drops, and you begin to **pick up the same kind of energy from others**. Thought energy is contagious, and we are more susceptible to its influence than we often realize.

We are, to a great degree, the **product of our repeated thought patterns**, combined with the influence of the thoughts and beliefs of others—whether they reach us through conversation or are silently transmitted through thought waves. However, our **dominant mental attitude** acts as a filter. It decides what kind of energy we receive and what kind we reject.

The thoughts that resonate with our inner state have the strongest effect. If we carry within us an attitude of strength and confidence, we naturally reject thoughts of discouragement and defeat. But if we are in a low state, those same negative thoughts can land more easily and pull us down even further.

The Law of Attraction works not only to project your thoughts outward, but also to attract inward the thoughts of others who are in alignment with you. If you're focused on growth and achievement, you'll find yourself connecting—consciously or not—with others who are also focused on the same. You'll feed each other's progress.

If your mind is always circling around failure, pessimism, and fear, you'll begin to pick up signals from others in the same mental loop, and together you'll sink further into it. Thought frequencies connect and reinforce one another. That's why people who expect the worst often find more reasons to be proven right—because **they're unconsciously seeking and tuning into it**.

We tend to see what we expect to see. Our thoughts filter reality. If you go through life looking for goodness, opportunity, and strength, you'll discover that these things were always around you—you were just finally ready to receive them.

Think of a radio or a wireless receiver, like Marconi's early telegraph system. It only responds to signals from a transmitter that is tuned to the same frequency. All kinds of signals may be flying through the air around it, but **only those on the right frequency make the receiver vibrate**. The same principle applies to your mind.

If you're feeling down, anxious, or frustrated, it's a sign you've allowed your internal frequency to drop. When that happens, you not only echo your own negative thoughts—you begin to pick up the heavy, discouraging energy sent out by others operating on that same level. Without realizing it, you've entered a frequency field that deepens your state and feeds itself.

On the other hand, the moment you shift into a state of enthusiasm, courage, or focused determination, you rise to a different level—and **you instantly begin to receive powerful, uplifting energy** from others tuned to that same vibration.

This isn't just metaphor—it's observable in everyday life. You can often feel the emotional charge of a person just by entering a room. Some people energize you with their presence, while others drain you without saying a word. That same transfer of mental energy happens even when you're physically apart, just at a lower intensity.

The human mind can operate at countless levels of "pitch," from the highest, most positive mental states, down to the lowest, most passive or negative ones. Every thought you think places you somewhere along that scale.

When you're thinking at a high mental frequency, you feel alive, capable, optimistic, and confident. You become magnetic. You influence others, attract opportunity, and lead with natural force. Your thought waves are strong, clear, and contagious.

But when you fall into the lowest end of the scale—worry, fear, resentment, passivity—you feel weak and unable to act. You become influenced by others rather than influencing them. You may find yourself being used, overlooked, or pushed aside by those operating at stronger frequencies.

Some people naturally radiate more positivity, while others seem to stay stuck in a negative tone. But it's important to realize that **your mental frequency is never fixed**. You may be "negative" to one person while being "positive" in relation to someone else. Mental relationships are dynamic and constantly shifting.

Every time two people meet, a **silent energetic negotiation takes place**. Their minds unconsciously measure each other's strength. Often the outcome is subtle, automatic—but sometimes the energies are so closely matched that you feel an intense friction, like magnets resisting one another.

In some cases, two people never find alignment because their frequencies constantly clash. They may remain in conflict, compete, or eventually drift apart. In other cases, one person adjusts to match the other's energy—either rising up or being pulled down.

You are constantly either leading or being led, influencing or being influenced. You might be the confident parent at home, but a passive subordinate at work. These relationships shift based on how we perceive ourselves and how we allow others to influence our frequency.

Sometimes, something awakens in us, and we suddenly begin radiating a stronger, clearer signal than ever before. This inner awakening changes our relationship dynamics. The more you learn about thought energy and mental law, the more frequently you'll experience this kind of internal transformation.

The good news is that you always have the power to raise your own frequency. Through focused will, **you can tune your mind to a higher pitch**. You can rise out of a negative slump by intentionally shifting your thoughts and emotions toward something stronger. But just as easily, you can drop into negativity by neglecting your inner state or allowing outside influences to dictate your vibration.

It's true that the world is filled with more negative thought energy than positive—but here's the key: **a single positive thought is far more powerful** than dozens of negative ones. If you can keep yourself tuned to the higher frequency, you'll naturally repel negativity and draw in waves of encouragement, clarity, and inner strength.

This is one of the secrets behind affirmations and self-suggestions used in many modern mental training programs. The affirmations themselves aren't magical—but they help shift your inner state. They raise your vibration and reprogram your thinking.

Affirmations work in two ways:

1. They begin to rewrite your mental patterns and build up a new internal identity.
2. They put your mind on a frequency that attracts more thoughts—and people—who resonate with your new direction.

Even when we don't realize it, we're always affirming something. If you tell yourself "I can do this," with conviction, you spark a wave of internal support and unlock mental resources to help you succeed. You also tune into the mental waves of others who are focused on confidence and achievement.

But if you constantly say "I can't," "I'll fail," or "Nothing works," you shut down your own inner power and start aligning with the mental frequencies of failure, fear, and defeat. These thought forms are abundant in the world—and they're always available for you to tune into, if you allow yourself.

The lesson here is simple: **be intentional with your thoughts**. Don't passively absorb the negative energy around you. Instead, rise above it. Elevate your mental frequency and connect with the higher current of strong, positive thought energy being transmitted by others who are on the same path.

My purpose throughout this book is to help you train your mind and **develop your will**, so you can command your inner state and raise your mental pitch whenever necessary. You don't have to operate at maximum energy all the time—that would be exhausting. Instead, learn to keep your baseline frequency high and steady, so you can quickly rise when the situation calls for it.

Once you gain this control, you'll no longer be subject to the automatic swings of emotion or influence. You'll steer your mental state deliberately, like a captain guiding a ship.

Building your mental will is just like building a muscle—it takes **repetition, effort, and time**. At first it may feel forced, but every attempt strengthens you. Eventually, the state that once required effort becomes your natural default.

We've all had moments when we "rose to the occasion," suddenly finding strength or clarity in an emergency. Imagine making that your **everyday mindset**. With consistent practice, you can raise your normal state to match that level—and then take it even further when needed.

That doesn't mean living in constant high intensity. In fact, **rest and receptivity are essential**. There are times when you'll need to relax and absorb new ideas or emotions. When you're in a receptive state, you're learning. When you're in a positive, active state, you're teaching or creating.

True mastery means knowing when to **step forward and when to listen**, when to transmit and when to receive.

Let this be your goal: to maintain control over your mental pitch, to stay balanced, and to rise to your highest frequency whenever life requires it.

Chapter 3: **The Dual Nature of the Mind**

Every person has one mind—but that single mind is made up of many distinct **mental faculties**, each with the ability to function in two main ways. These functions aren't separated by hard boundaries; instead, they flow into each other like the subtle transitions between colors in a rainbow.

Each mental faculty can operate through what we might call an **Active mode** or a **Passive mode**. The Active mode is triggered by conscious effort—it's fresh, intentional, and generated in the moment. The Passive mode, by contrast, is reactive or automatic. It's the result of prior activity—whether from our own past thoughts, external suggestion, influence from others' thought waves, or even subconscious impulses passed down through generations.

To simplify: **Active thought is present-moment creation**, while Passive thought is old programming replaying itself—either from your own past or inherited from external forces. When you make an Active mental effort, you're forging a new trail. When you rely on the Passive mode, you're walking the old, familiar path that's already been carved out.

This is important, because once a thought or action is repeated often enough, it becomes **a habit**, continuing on its own momentum. A thought that started with conscious choice may soon run automatically, like a wheel that keeps spinning after being set in motion. Over time, the force behind it builds, making it harder to change direction unless a **new Active effort** steps in to reroute or stop it.

The Active mind has the power to **launch**, **modify**, or **cancel** any mental process. It can reinforce a thought pattern, reshape it, or replace it with a stronger one. Once launched, thought-impulses continue vibrating in Passive mode unless they are altered by a fresh, directed effort from your conscious will.

This is the secret behind why habits—mental, emotional, or behavioral—are often so hard to break. Their strength doesn't come from one powerful thought, but from **thousands of repetitions** powered by Passive momentum. The same law explains why positive habits become effortless over time: their initial effort gave birth to a pattern, and the pattern began to run itself.

Of course, any habit—good or bad—can be rewritten. The Active mind has the authority to override the Passive, to neutralize unhelpful patterns and build new ones in their place. The key is intention, consistency, and awareness.

In real-life situations, **multiple faculties of the mind often collaborate**. Let's say you're solving a problem: some parts of your mind may be working actively, while others are drawing from memory or habit, operating passively. New situations tend to demand more Active effort, while familiar routines can be handled on autopilot.

This built-in efficiency makes mental processing smoother—but it also has a downside: **it keeps old programming running**, even when we've outgrown it. That's why personal development often begins with the conscious decision to bring the Passive into awareness—and upgrade it.

At the root of all life, there exists a **natural tendency** in living organisms to pursue what fulfills them. This tendency—sometimes called **appetency**—is a Passive force, a kind of primal momentum set in motion by what we might call the Original Cause or Source. Over time, it's been passed down, shaped by evolution, growing stronger as consciousness has evolved.

You can see this force even in plants. From the simplest forms to the most complex, there's an unmistakable drive toward light, growth, and life. This is the **life-force**—not just biology, but the earliest signs of **mental activity**, even if in rudimentary form. In some higher plants, you'll even notice behaviors that resemble decision-making. These are the first flickers of Active mental energy.

In the **animal kingdom**, this progression continues. Passive mental action is highly developed, allowing creatures to operate by instinct with incredible precision. But we also see traces of **Active mentation**, especially in more intelligent species. Animals may not reason exactly like humans, but their volitional responses—their capacity to choose and act—sometimes match those of young children or humans in undeveloped states.

Just as the physical development of a child before birth reflects humanity's evolutionary stages, so too does the **mental development of a child** echo the gradual unfolding of consciousness through time. We watch them evolve from Passive instinct into Active will, one layer at a time.

Humans, at least as we know them, represent the highest stage of mental evolution on Earth. We possess not only deep Passive mental capacity—our memories, instincts, and habits—but also an expanded power for **Active thought**, the conscious shaping of ideas, choices, and beliefs. Yet, even among adults, there is a wide range in how much of this potential is realized.

Surprisingly, a person's level of **Active mental development has little to do with their social class, education, or even intelligence**. Culture and knowledge are not the same as mental strength. Mental Culture is about external input—books, information, rituals. Mental Development is about internal capacity—will, self-awareness, mental direction.

Look around, and you'll notice the difference immediately. Many people **don't actually think for themselves**. They operate almost entirely through Passive processes—reacting, following, repeating, complying. Active thinking feels difficult to them. It's easier to let someone else direct their mind than to lead it themselves. Their mental energy flows down the path of least resistance.

Among both animals and humans, the more material, basic faculties tend to dominate Active effort—fighting for food, survival, comfort. The higher mental powers—creativity, reason, intuition—often remain **Passive**, unless consciously awakened.

As species evolved, new faculties emerged from within, always beginning in **Passive form**. Over time, through repeated exposure and challenge, they were gradually drawn into **Active expression**. This is the pattern of all evolution: what is first instinctive becomes voluntary. What is first dormant becomes dynamic.

The process hasn't ended. In fact, **we're still evolving**—mentally, emotionally, and energetically. Humanity is now at a stage where **new mental powers are beginning to emerge**—intuition, empathy, spiritual perception. These begin passively, as subtle impressions, but some individuals have already learned to activate and direct them with conscious effort.

This is the foundation of many **Eastern and Western esoteric traditions**. The secret is not about gaining more power—it's about learning how to use what already exists within you.

The mind's ability to follow the will can be strengthened through **focused, repeated practice**. What we often refer to as "Willpower" is really just the ability of the mind to listen and respond to the **inner directive force**—the I AM, the real self beneath the surface thoughts. The Will is not weak; it's always flowing. What needs training is the mind's capacity to respond to it.

Imagine your Will as an electrical current running overhead. You don't need to generate it—it's already there. But you must learn to **raise the trolley pole** of your mind and make contact. Only then will your mental machinery begin to move forward.

This view of Willpower may differ from what you've heard before—but test it for yourself. If you experiment with this mindset—believing that Will is already available—you'll notice your ability to act, decide, and follow through will grow tremendously.

The upward pull of **the Absolute**, the highest intelligence or source of being, is always present. Combined with the lingering power of the original creative impulse—the Primal Cause—**you are being invited to rise**. Now more than ever, human beings are capable of helping themselves. Those who understand these laws and apply them can transform their lives in ways that seem miraculous to others.

Those who remain ignorant of these principles, or who reject them outright, may continue to suffer—not because of fate, but due to **disconnection from truth**. The truth doesn't punish—it simply waits to be used.

When you understand the mechanisms of your own mind, you begin to master your faculties. You use Passive mental energy where it fits—routine, repetition, memorization—and you save your Active mental effort for creation, leadership, transformation.

You do not fight your Passive mind; you **train it**, like a loyal assistant. You assign it the tasks that serve your purpose, knowing that with the right direction, it can produce extraordinary results. But you also know how to correct it when needed and avoid interfering with it blindly, which can cause more confusion than clarity.

In this balanced state, you start to **awaken your full potential**. You don't abandon old thought patterns—you reshape them. You don't reject instinct—you elevate it. You begin expressing higher and higher levels of consciousness, both instinctive and volitional.

You become the master of your own internal kingdom. Both the Passive and Active sides of your mind now serve your deeper self—the part of you that simply is. You're no longer ruled by fear or scattered desire. You've found clarity, direction, and freedom.

You've discovered something few ever do:
You've found the secret of the I AM.

Chapter 4: **Constructing the Mind from the Inside Out**

You have the power to shape your mind—to build it intentionally, to strengthen it with effort, and to refine it into an instrument that reflects your highest vision. Whether we realize it or not, we are all engaged in this process—**mind-building**—every hour of every day. Most people do it unconsciously, responding to the moment without ever questioning the internal structures they're reinforcing. But those who begin to awaken to the deeper nature of things take the process into their own hands.

They no longer leave their mental state at the mercy of outside influences or inherited patterns. They become **conscious architects** of their own mentality. They take the driver's seat. Instead of being shaped by moods, thoughts, and desires, they learn to **direct** them.

This shift begins when you recognize your true identity—the **inner "I"**—the part of you that chooses, observes, commands. This "I" is the rightful ruler of the mental kingdom, and **your Will** is its tool, the means through which it expresses authority. Yes, there is a greater Universal Will that encompasses all, and ultimately your individual will is an extension of that universal force. But the moment you step into the fullness of your self—when you claim your inner power—you begin to **realign** with the Universal Will. You become a conscious participant in its flow.

Yet before you can access this immense power, you must first **conquer the scattered parts of yourself**—the lower tendencies, impulses, and patterns that have taken control.

It's a contradiction to imagine you can wield great power while being enslaved by your own emotions, cravings, or reactions. How can someone who's governed by anger, jealousy, or fear ever hope to express strength, peace, or mastery? These qualities cannot coexist.

And to be clear, this is not about asceticism or repression. It's not about denying the body or silencing all desires. That path often leads to imbalance. What we're talking about is **Self-Mastery**—the ability to bring every part of your being into harmony under the guidance of your conscious self.

In truth, the "I"—the observing, willing, sovereign self—is the **only true you**. Everything else—the moods, the thoughts, the emotional waves—is secondary. But for now, we'll refer to the whole of you, including these parts, as the "self," for simplicity. The goal is to **reorganize** that self so that the Real You is in command.

Until the higher self takes control, the lower parts will continue running the show. Habits, appetites, emotional impulses—they'll keep making decisions for you, unless you step in and take the reins. **Everything has its rightful place**, but when lower aspects dominate, chaos and imbalance follow.

You've likely seen this in your own life. You know what it's like to feel governed by stress, to be pulled into habits you know don't serve you, to feel trapped in emotional loops. That's what happens when the **inner King or Queen is off the throne**.

If you've been living this way, know that you're not being judged—it's simply a stage of growth. But if you're ready for the next step, **the moment to take control is now**.

You've let inner rebels—the lesser urges and undisciplined thoughts—hold the throne long enough. You've let Fear dictate your decisions, let Overindulgence weaken your body, let Doubt cloud your vision. It's time to reclaim your mental sovereignty.

The good news is that you already possess the authority. **You can command any inner force**—emotion, appetite, thought—into submission through the focused use of Will. You can say to Fear: "Step aside." You can command Anger to quiet itself, Worry to dissolve, and Impulse to bow. With the same Will, you can welcome qualities like Calm, Confidence, Love, and Discipline into your presence. They are available the moment you invite them—and enforce your authority.

Before you can lead in the world, you must establish **internal order**. Before you can build outward success, you must build inner stability. The first battle is always the most important: the **victory of the true self over the conditioned self**.

AFFIRMATION

I Am Asserting the Mastery of My Real Self

Repeat these words often—clearly, consciously, and with intention. Let them become a guiding force throughout your day. Say them especially in moments of weakness, when you're tempted to act from fear or habit instead of strength and clarity.

Say them aloud when doubt creeps in. Let them anchor you when you feel indecision or emotional noise rising. Visualize your higher self—clear, focused, wise—rising to take command. Picture this version of you stepping forward and taking the throne.

Before sleep, repeat this affirmation slowly and with feeling. But remember, **don't just say the words mechanically**. Back them with belief. Let them awaken a vivid image in your mind: your truest self, steady and sovereign, bringing peace and purpose to every part of your inner life.

You'll begin to feel a new current stirring within you. Things that used to feel difficult will start to feel easier. Your sense of personal power will increase. You'll walk with greater presence. And you'll know—deeply—that **you are the master, not the slave**.

EXERCISE

Whenever you feel pulled by emotion or tempted by reaction, bring your attention inward. Pause. And then—**assert the "I."**

If anger rises, speak firmly within: "I do not choose anger. I choose clarity." And notice how your tone softens.

If irritation or restlessness surfaces, say: "I remember who I am." Step above the moment. Anchor yourself in the higher self.

If fear knocks, remind yourself: "My true self knows no fear." Stand tall. Let courage step in.

When jealousy, envy, or insecurity begin to surface, laugh gently. Remember that those thoughts come from the lesser self—and they **do not define you**. Affirm your higher nature.

Each time you catch yourself and redirect the moment, you're strengthening the pathway from Passive reaction to Active control. You're teaching your mind and emotions their proper roles—not as masters, but as loyal servants.

You may stumble in the beginning. That's natural. You're undoing years—maybe decades—of automatic response. But if you persist, something remarkable will happen: **your inner world will transform**.

You'll no longer be tossed around by shifting moods. You'll no longer be trapped by craving or guilt. You'll feel calm even when others aren't. You'll experience freedom where once there was inner chaos.

You've lived long enough in mental servitude. **Now is the time to step into your inner throne.**

If you follow this process consistently—if you practice these exercises with sincerity—you will be a different person in a matter of months. You'll look back on your current struggles not with shame, but with understanding and compassion, knowing that they were part of your awakening.

But know this: **it requires effort**. This is not a casual experiment. It's a commitment. The journey of Self-Mastery is for those who are ready to claim their full potential.

The question is:

Will you make the effort?

Chapter 5: **Unlocking the Secret of Willpower**

Experts in psychology may disagree on how the Will functions or what it truly is—but no one denies its existence, nor questions its power. Everyone recognizes that **strong Willpower** has the ability to break through resistance, defy odds, and reshape lives. We've all seen people use it to overcome enormous challenges.

Yet, surprisingly, very few understand that this powerful force can be **strengthened and cultivated** through deliberate, focused practice. Many people say, "If only I had more Willpower, I could change everything." But instead of taking steps to develop it, they sink into passive frustration. They sigh, complain, and remain stuck.

Those who've truly explored the subject of Will know that it is not some random gift reserved for the lucky few. **Willpower is a force of nature**, and like any other energy—like fire, electricity, or steam—it can be harnessed, directed, and amplified through conscious training. You don't need to fully understand its origins to benefit from its effects. Regardless of the theory you accept, **results come from application**.

Personally, I hold a unique view. I believe that everyone already has **a deep well of Willpower within them**—a reservoir waiting to be tapped. I don't think we need to build Will so much as we need to **learn how to use what's already there**. In the higher levels of consciousness, I believe a powerful current of Will is always flowing. The key is learning how to **raise your mental contact point—your "trolley pole"—and make connection with that current**.

Imagine you're connected to an infinite power source. The Universal Will is that source. Your individual Will is not separate—it's simply an expression of that higher force. When your mental system is refined, aligned, and focused, the Will flows through it with great strength. When the system is blocked, scattered, or out of tune, the current weakens—not because the Will itself has disappeared, but because your mind isn't receiving it properly.

You may or may not agree with that theory. And that's perfectly fine. What matters most is this: **the practice works**. Whether you believe Willpower is internal or universal, fixed or fluid, doesn't matter. When you train your mind to cooperate with Will, your life transforms.

Those who've developed their mental faculties to **channel Will effectively** have discovered a gateway to extraordinary potential. They gain not just energy or confidence—they awaken latent abilities and strengths they didn't even know existed. The Will becomes a **key that unlocks new doors** in every area of life.

As the writer Donald G. Mitchell once said: "Resolve is what makes a man manifest... not vague wishes, but that firm, unshakable Will which crushes resistance like boots across frosty ground." A strong Will ignites purpose, lifts our gaze toward the impossible, and makes giants out of ordinary people.

We all know what it feels like to think, *"If only I had the Will to do this, I could accomplish anything."* And yet, we rarely act. We procrastinate, avoid discomfort, and convince ourselves we'll begin "someday." That day never comes—because **desire without action** is just a dream.

Many of us can feel the **potential power of Will** bubbling beneath the surface. But we lack the focus or urgency to use it. We let life carry us along, unless pain or hardship forces us into motion. Sometimes, a crisis pushes us to take control. At other times, we wait, hoping motivation will strike. But motivation doesn't always come. Sometimes, the only way forward is to **act first and feel later**.

The real problem is not a lack of Willpower—it's a lack of **intensity of desire**. We don't want the thing badly enough. Our thoughts are divided. We are mentally lazy. And when the desire is weak, the Will stays dormant.

If you're uncomfortable with the word "desire," replace it with "aspiration." Some people prefer to distinguish between "desire" for lower wants and "aspiration" for higher goals. Use whichever term resonates with you. Either way, the message is clear: **Will follows deep want**. When something matters enough, the Will awakens.

We've all witnessed sudden bursts of Willpower. A woman facing danger to her child can lift weights she couldn't normally budge. A man facing disaster can suddenly act with clarity and strength. A boy will work for hours if it's play—but can't lift a finger if the task is dull. The Will shows up when **emotion and intention** are aligned.

So if you've been telling yourself that you "can't" do something, it's time to be honest. Ask yourself: *Do I really want this? Or do I want something else more?* Often, we claim to want change, but we aren't willing to pay the price. We prefer the comfort of the known, even if it limits us.

Take a moment to reflect. This is where true progress begins. Once you stop blaming your Will and start **clarifying your priorities**, you unlock the real source of change.

Let's be blunt: **your Will is not weak—your mind is undisciplined**. You have a powerful storehouse of Will within you, but you've been too mentally lazy to activate it. If you truly want to change, then stop talking and start choosing. Define your goal, then begin. The Will will be there **when you commit fully**.

The turning point is not in some distant future—it's in the **moment of decision**. Once you resolve, fully and deeply, to move in a certain direction, Willpower becomes available. The universe seems to respond to clarity of intention.

Much has been written about the greatness of Willpower. Many books exalt it, call it the master force, the tool of transformation. And they're right. But surprisingly few explain **how to actually develop it**. Some offer exercises to "strengthen the Will," but these exercises actually train the **mind**—preparing it to receive the Will more clearly.

In fact, the real secret to Will development lies in **autosuggestion**—in consistently reminding yourself of your inner capacity, in planting thoughts of power, control, and determination in the soil of your mind. These suggestions prepare the ground, allowing Will to grow and take root.

AUTOSUGGESTION

I Am Using My Willpower

Say these words clearly, confidently, and with intention—**right now**. Repeat them several times throughout the day, especially when you feel resistance. Say them again before bed, letting the thought settle into your subconscious as you sleep.

But remember—**the words alone mean nothing** if you don't fill them with meaning. The power is in the thought behind the phrase. The words are anchors—tools for the deeper work. As you speak them, visualize your Will rising within you like a wave. Feel its presence. Let the phrase become a trigger for action.

At first, you may need **faith**. You might not feel powerful yet. That's okay. Just begin with belief, even if it feels fragile. As you keep repeating the thought, the feeling will grow. You'll notice shifts. Suddenly, things that once seemed difficult will feel doable. Old habits will loosen their grip. Your confidence will grow.

You'll feel a new kind of **energy stirring within you**—one that pushes through hesitation, bypasses excuses, and reaches for what matters. It's not magic—it's Will.

EXERCISE

Do one unpleasant or difficult task **every day** for the next month. Choose something you've been avoiding. It could be small—washing dishes, organizing papers, making that phone call. But it must be something you normally resist.

Why? Not because this will make you meek or self-sacrificing. **This is a Willpower workout.** Anyone can do what they like. True strength is built by doing what you'd rather avoid—and doing it **with purpose and grace**.

This single practice will reshape your relationship with discomfort. After a month, you'll feel a new resilience. You'll trust yourself more. You'll realize that **you can do hard things**.

But if you skip this—if you read these words and then shrug and move on—be honest: you're not really committed to change. You're still making excuses. And that's fine, if you're okay staying where you are.

But if you're serious—if you want to rise above your current limitations—then start today. Pick something small. Do it. Do it **even if you don't want to**. Especially if you don't want to.

That's how Will is born. That's how giants are made.

Chapter 6: How to Become Immune to Negative Thought Influence

The first step toward freeing yourself from harmful mental influence is simple, but crucial: **cut out fear and worry**. These two forms of thought are among the most destructive forces we deal with. You've probably heard that before—but it bears repeating. Fear is a habit—a pattern that most people have unconsciously absorbed through cultural conditioning and generations of negative thinking. But like all habits, **it can be broken**, and your freedom lies in that truth.

Fear, more than anything, is what keeps people from living fully. It's what kills dreams before they begin and paralyzes us when we most need to act. On the flip side, **expectation and trust** in a positive outcome act like magnets. When you want something deeply and confidently—with calm hope and certainty—you begin to attract the people, ideas, and circumstances that move you in that direction.

But this law doesn't discriminate. It works just as powerfully when your mind is filled with fear. When you expect danger, failure, or disappointment, you unconsciously start building the path toward it. Why? Because fear is a form of belief. When you **fear something**, you are mentally **expecting it**—and energetically inviting it.

So here's the truth: the law of attraction responds to emotional energy, not just conscious wishes. And in the eyes of that law, **expecting something bad is no different from wanting it**. The force is the same—the direction is different. That's why fear must be eliminated at the root.

Now, how do you fight fear? The answer may surprise you: **you don't fight it directly**. Just like you don't banish darkness by struggling with it—you simply **turn on the light**. The most effective way to overcome fear is by intentionally activating the opposite quality: **Courage**.

Don't waste time trying to suppress fear through force. That's like shouting at a shadow to disappear. Instead, fill your mental space with the energy of courage. Think about courage. Speak about courage. Imagine yourself as courageous. And gradually, the light of courage will displace the shadow of fear.

So instead of repeating, "I'm not afraid," say boldly, **"I am courageous"** or **"I am filled with courage."** Don't focus on fear at all—just focus on strengthening the mindset that renders fear powerless.

You become what you think about consistently. So if you want to remove fear, **replace it with courage in thought, word, and action**. Keep your mental vision fixed on what it means to be brave, calm, and confident. Visualize yourself responding to difficult situations with steadiness. Practice this mental picture until it becomes your default reaction.

Let the word "Courage" sink deep into your subconscious. Let it echo in your mind throughout the day. The more you focus on this image of strength, the more your brain and nervous system will adapt to match it. You'll notice your emotional responses beginning to change. What once triggered you will no longer feel threatening. You'll start moving through life with more ease and clarity.

The person who is confident, fearless, and expectant becomes a **magnet** for success. He draws opportunities and support. Things seem to "work out" for him, not because of luck, but because of alignment. This kind of mental attitude transforms not only the person—but also the environment around him.

Compare that to someone ruled by fear. Even if they have talent or resources, their inner doubt holds them back. Their negative mindset attracts other fearful people and situations. The fearful mind restricts potential, while the confident mind **activates it**.

Think of someone you admire—someone who achieves, inspires, or leads. Odds are, that person doesn't operate from fear. They carry themselves with a quiet certainty, an "I Can and I Will" mindset. That energy is magnetic. And it's not something you're either born with or without—it's something you **develop**.

You can choose that mindset too. You can live on the "I Can and I Will" frequency. Start today. Think it. Speak it. Move from it. Dream from it. Act from it. The results may start subtle, but over time, you'll feel them—**in your choices, your emotions, your energy, and your outcomes**.

Let go of "what if I fail?" and replace it with "what if I fly?"

Fear is the root from which many other problems grow. Worry, anger, jealousy, resentment, self-sabotage—they all stem from fear. Remove fear, and you cut off the fuel that powers them. You'll find yourself calmer, clearer, and more capable.

Getting rid of fear is the **first major milestone** in the path to mental mastery. As long as fear is running the show, you won't be able to use your mental powers at their highest capacity. It will cloud your decisions, drain your strength, and limit your actions.

So here's the challenge: **start now**. Make the decision to confront and uproot fear. Don't try to negotiate with it. Don't make room for it. Declare that fear no longer belongs in your life. You may not be able to remove it all at once—but each time you act from courage, fear gets smaller.

Each time you stand up to fear, it loses power. **Stop feeding it**. Starve it of attention. Starve it of belief. Fear cannot survive in a mind filled with thoughts of power and possibility.

Remember: fear is **passive**, weak, and unoriginal. It doesn't create—it only reacts. Courage, on the other hand, is active. It builds. It leads. It elevates. And in the end, the positive will always overpower the negative.

Fear sneaks in with words like "but," "what if," "I can't," "suppose," or "I'm afraid." These are its weapons. And as long as they're in your vocabulary, they're anchoring your thoughts. Remove them. Replace them with decisive, empowering language.

Once you remove fear, you'll be shocked at how **fluid and free your thinking becomes**. Obstacles will seem smaller. Opportunities will feel closer. Your Thought Energy will begin to flow more freely, without being blocked or diffused by hesitation.

So here's a suggestion: start doing the very things you've been **avoiding out of fear**. Pick something small at first—something you've told yourself you can't do. Do it anyway. Affirm courage as you act. Say it aloud: "I am Courageous." And notice how your perception changes.

You'll discover that most of the difficulty was in the anticipation—not in the act itself. The mental fog of fear distorted your view, but **once you step into action, the fog clears**.

This kind of self-directed challenge is one of the best practices you can undertake. It builds character. It expands your comfort zone. And each time you complete such an act, your inner strength grows visibly.

There is **so much waiting for you**—so many goals, experiences, and relationships—that are just on the other side of fear. The only thing keeping them from you is a mental wall you've agreed to maintain. Refuse to keep holding it up. Let it crumble.

You are not here to live in mental confinement. You are here to **express your full strength**, to walk with dignity, and to manifest the vision you carry deep inside. That begins with one decision: the decision to let courage lead.

Don't wait for fear to disappear before you act. Act—and fear will disappear.

AFFIRMATION

I am Courageous. I am Fearless. I am the Master of my Mind.

Repeat these words when fear arises. Repeat them when things feel uncertain. Speak them with strength—not just in voice, but in intention. Let them rewire the inner dialogue that's been shaped by fear. You are not your past reactions. You are who you choose to be now.

EXERCISE

Pick one thing you've been avoiding—something fear has kept you from attempting. It could be speaking up, applying for something, taking a risk, or setting a boundary. Now, **do it**. Prepare yourself with calm, strong thoughts. Repeat your affirmation. Visualize yourself succeeding. Then take the action.

Each successful confrontation with fear is **a massive victory**. Over time, your mind will begin to register these actions as normal. Courage will become your default mode. Your baseline will rise. And what once intimidated you will now inspire you.

Bring the word "Courage" with you everywhere. Let it be your mental compass and your emotional anchor.

Because in the end, the only real thing to fear... is fear itself.

And even fear **runs** from someone who stands tall and says:

"I am ready. I am able. I am fearless."

Chapter 7 - Transforming Worry into Power

Worry, that persistent and corrosive mental habit, is the direct offspring of fear. If fear is the root, worry is the fruit it bears—anxiety, restlessness, unease, and paralysis. And if we truly want to eliminate worry from our lives, the most effective way is to starve it at its source by uprooting fear entirely. This truth has been stated countless times throughout history, and yet, like a vital medicine we keep forgetting to take, it bears repeating over and over again until it becomes a part of our internal blueprint for living.

Now, there are those who argue—sometimes quite vocally—that worry is essential to achievement. That without it, we'd become lazy, indifferent, unmotivated. I've even come across articles in reputable publications insisting that worry is what fuels accomplishment, that it's the spark that drives ambition. But I must respectfully—and firmly—disagree. No matter how intelligent or educated the voice saying it may be, the idea that worry is productive is a dangerous fallacy.

Worry is not the driving force behind human achievement. It is, in truth, a hindrance. The real engines of progress, of action, of creation, are Desire and Interest—those vital inner currents that stir us toward the things we value and long to experience. When you genuinely desire something, when your interest in attaining it is strong and unwavering, your entire mental system responds accordingly. Ideas begin to rise to the surface. Your subconscious mind becomes engaged in solving problems for you, even when you're unaware of it. It scans the landscape of your thoughts and experiences and draws forth solutions, strategies, and resources, all oriented toward helping you fulfill that desire.

Worry does not do that. Worry freezes the creative faculties. Worry wrings its hands and groans. It clouds the mind. It tightens the chest. It whispers of failure but offers no solutions. Desire, by contrast, sharpens the senses. It clarifies the mind. It stirs the blood and energizes the body. When you desire something deeply, and your interest is aligned with that desire, it is as though every fiber of your being is oriented toward your goal. And that, not worry, is the beginning of true change.

Now, to be clear, desperation can also lead to action. When a person's life becomes so intolerable that they can no longer endure it, they may finally rise up and do something about it. But that surge of energy does not come from worry—it comes from the desire for something better. It is the same force, only ignited under pressure. The man who says, "I cannot live like this anymore—I must change"—he is not acting from worry. He is acting from a burning desire to be free, to grow, to evolve.

And here's the transformation: when that desire becomes strong enough, it transmutes worry into action. It takes the restless energy of fear and repurposes it into movement. The man or woman becomes consumed with interest. Their mind lights up with possibility. They begin to think creatively, to take steps, to look for opportunities. And as they do this, something beautiful occurs—they begin to draw to themselves the very things they need.

Yes, truly, when you transmute worry into focused desire and trust in your own ability, the mind begins to operate like a magnet. Thoughts of value arise. People and situations are drawn to you. You become attuned to opportunities you might have missed before. This isn't just poetic language—it's a law of nature, a law of energy.

You see, our minds are like tuning forks. Whatever frequency we hold within us—whether fear or confidence, worry or desire—we attract more of the same. A person who is consumed by worry and doubt sends out those vibrations, and life responds in kind. But the person whose thoughts are rich with interest, clarity, and intention becomes a magnetic field for solutions, resources, and help. The universe moves in their favor because they've moved into alignment with its higher order.

The Law of Attraction—often mocked by skeptics and misunderstood by many—is not a fairy tale. It is a profound principle, one that has been demonstrated countless times by those who dare to test it. When your dominant thoughts are focused, passionate, and energized by strong desire, you initiate a powerful chain of events. Your actions change. Your posture changes. Your interactions change. And you find that people, ideas, and circumstances begin to support your path in ways you never expected.

But desire must be strong. Lukewarm wishes do not summon the same force. If you want to truly activate this power within you, you must want your goal more than the distractions and comforts that hold you back. And you must be willing to let go of the lesser desires that compete with the greater one. You must sometimes trade short-term ease for long-term growth. Are you prepared to do that?

If not, then ask yourself: do I truly want what I say I want? Do I desire it with the same passion that a drowning man desires air? With the same intensity that a prisoner desires freedom? Because history and experience both tell us that when desire reaches that level, mountains move. Obstacles crumble. Locked doors swing open.

Worry, on the other hand, is the great paralyzer. It kills desire. It stifles initiative. It shrinks the mind until even simple decisions become unbearable. I've had moments in my life where worry gripped me so tightly that it seemed as though all the color drained from the world. Hope faded. Enthusiasm disappeared. I felt weak, incapable, and lost. But when I finally faced those fears head-on, when I chose to stand up and reclaim my power, the clouds began to lift. Answers came. Strength returned. The challenge either faded away or revealed a hidden path through it.

You've probably experienced the same thing. We all have. That moment when you decide, once and for all, to face what you've been avoiding. And then—miraculously—it's no longer as overwhelming as it seemed.

So why waste energy worrying about what might happen? Most of the things we dread never come to pass. And those that do are often milder than we feared. What's more, they usually arrive hand in hand with new insights, unexpected allies, and inner strength we didn't know we had. Life tends to balance itself. There is pain, yes—but there is also healing. There is resistance, but also growth.

So rather than pouring your energy into imaginary catastrophes, save that energy. Preserve your strength for the real challenges—and you'll find you're more than equipped to handle them when they arrive.

The truth is, we don't overcome difficulty by worrying about it. We overcome it by thinking clearly, acting with courage, and remaining open to possibility. So, don't wait for tomorrow's imagined problems to paralyze you. Stay rooted in today. Focus your energy on what's right in front of you. Concentrate on progress, on solutions, on steps forward, no matter how small.

This is the great secret: the mind can only hold one dominant thought at a time. If you fill it with positive, focused intention, the worry has no room to stay. You cannot think of courage and fear at the same time. You must choose. And the more you choose courage, the stronger it becomes.

Every time you interrupt a worry spiral with a clear, confident affirmation—such as "I can and I will"—you strengthen your mental resolve. You're not just saying words. You're changing your inner chemistry. You're shifting your emotional climate. And over time, your dominant mental state becomes one of strength instead of fear.

So I challenge you to test this for yourself. The next time worry creeps in, don't fight it directly. Instead, redirect your attention toward something meaningful. Focus on something that excites you, that empowers you. Begin building a vision of what you want—not what you fear.

And finally, remember this: worry cannot exist in a mind that is saturated with purposeful action. The more you fill your mind with determination, hope, confidence, and creative focus, the less room there is for fear. Eventually, it fades like mist in the morning sun.

Take "Courage" as your personal motto. Let it guide your thoughts, your decisions, your reactions. And as you do, you will begin to transform every worry into energy—every doubt into determination—every obstacle into opportunity.

Chapter 8 The Law of Mental Control

Your thoughts, whether you realize it or not, are constantly at work. They are never idle, never truly at rest. And here lies the secret so often overlooked: your thoughts can either act as loyal servants, faithfully executing your will and intentions, or they can become unruly tyrants, leading you in circles, exhausting your energy, and sabotaging your potential. The outcome depends not on the nature of thought itself, but on the way you choose to relate to your thinking. Will you take command of your mental faculties, or will you allow them to take command of you?

This is a decision that must be made consciously, for it does not happen by accident. To allow your mind to operate without direction is like handing over the reins of a powerful horse to a child. The horse will run wherever it pleases, often into danger, often into exhaustion, and very seldom in the direction of your choosing. But when the rider knows how to hold the reins firmly—how to steer, guide, and calm the restless animal—then the journey becomes purposeful. The destination is reached.

We are, every one of us, the engineers of a most intricate and miraculous machine—our mind. But sadly, most people have never studied its mechanics, never read its manual, and so they let it sputter and spin, wasting fuel, overheating, and wearing itself down through misuse and overuse. In truth, the vast majority of people are governed by thoughts they never consciously invited, reacting to mental habits inherited from others, or absorbed unknowingly from the world around them. These thought patterns become automatic, unconscious, persistent—and in many cases, destructive.

Yet, there is another way.

The key to mastering this incredible mental machine lies in a single word: concentration. Concentration is not about tightening the muscles or furrowing the brow in effort; it is about the deliberate direction of attention. It is about choosing what to focus on, holding that focus with gentle firmness, and returning to it whenever the mind tries to wander. Just as the sun's rays can be concentrated through a magnifying glass to produce heat, so too can the scattered light of your attention be focused to produce insight, clarity, and power.

When you learn to concentrate your mind, you will find that your work becomes easier and more efficient. You will no longer waste hours "thinking" while making little progress. Instead, you'll be able to zero in on the task at hand, using every ounce of your mental energy constructively, without resistance or distraction. And what's more—your mind will continue working even after you consciously stop. Many of our greatest ideas, solutions, and creative breakthroughs arrive during moments of rest, when the subconscious mind is allowed to process what the conscious mind has handed over.

Have you ever gone to bed troubled by a problem and awakened with a solution? That is no accident. That is the power of a trained mind operating in harmony with natural law. But to benefit from this invisible cooperation, you must learn not only how to think when necessary, but how to stop thinking when it's time to rest.

Mental control is not merely about productivity or problem-solving; it is also about peace. Imagine, for a moment, a machine that continues to run at full speed long after the job is done. The parts grind, the gears wear down, and the whole structure begins to shake from stress. That is exactly what happens to your mind when you cannot—or do not—learn how to pause your thinking.

There is a time for mental action, and there is a time for mental stillness. The wise person learns to recognize both. At the end of a day's effort, the mind should be allowed to cool. The fire should be gently banked, not extinguished, but allowed to simmer quietly, gathering strength for the work of tomorrow. Many people, however, keep feeding the fire. They lie awake at night turning over problems they cannot solve until morning. They rehash conversations, regrets, worries, and plans. They believe this is being responsible or productive, but in truth, it is the opposite. It is a misuse of energy. It is like driving a car in neutral—burning fuel without getting anywhere.

And how do we slow the mind? How do we bring the runaway engine to a gentle stop?

The secret lies in displacement. When a negative or restless thought occupies the mind, the answer is not to wrestle with it, trying to force it out. That only gives it more power. The more you fight a thought, the more you focus on it. And the more you focus on it, the stronger it becomes. The mind does not understand the language of resistance—it understands the language of replacement. You cannot stop thinking about "the thing" by repeating "I must not think of the thing." You stop thinking of it by choosing something else to think about and placing all of your attention there.

Think of your mind like a stage. Only one actor can stand in the spotlight at a time. If the wrong actor is on stage, don't yell at him to leave. Simply bring on the right one, place him in the spotlight, and the other will fade into the background.

This is not difficult to practice, although it may take time to perfect. At first, the mind may rebel. It may insist on returning to the old thought, the worry, the regret, the fear. That is normal. The mind is simply following the habit patterns it has learned. But just as a path in the woods becomes clearer with repeated walking, so too do new mental habits become stronger with repeated effort.

When you consciously choose your thoughts, day after day, moment after moment, you will soon find that the mind begins to follow your lead naturally. It becomes obedient, flexible, and responsive. It becomes a servant once more—not a tyrant. It goes where you point it, stays where you put it, and returns quickly when it wanders. This is the power of mental discipline.

There is another advantage to mastering the art of mental focus: it builds emotional stability. Emotions often follow thoughts. If your mind is filled with chaotic, fearful, or self-defeating ideas, your emotions will follow. Anxiety, insecurity, anger, sadness—these are not just feelings that "happen" to you. They are the natural consequences of ungoverned thinking. But when your thoughts are calm, clear, and constructive, your emotional life stabilizes. You feel more in control of yourself—not just your thoughts, but your moods, your reactions, your entire state of being.

There will still be moments of turbulence, of course. Life is full of unexpected winds and storms. But when the inner compass is strong—when the hand on the mental wheel is steady—you will not be thrown off course so easily. You will recover more quickly. You will sail through the storm, rather than sink beneath it.

To summarize: your thoughts are your tools. They are not your masters. You have been given this mind not as a burden, but as a gift. It is not meant to torment you, but to serve you. The secret lies in training it—teaching it where to go, what to do, and when to stop. This is not an overnight process. It is not something you do once and then forget. Like any skill, it must be practiced. But the rewards are immeasurable.

With mental control, you gain time. You gain energy. You gain peace. You stop wasting hours in useless thinking. You stop letting fear and worry hijack your days. You begin to live with intention, focus, and power. You begin to *create* rather than *react*. You begin to act from the center of your being, not from the chaos of your surroundings.

And so, I leave you with a challenge:

Tonight, when you lie down to rest, notice what your mind does. If it starts to race, if it stirs up tomorrow's worries or yesterday's regrets, gently bring it back. Guide it toward a quiet, pleasant thought—a beautiful place, a calming image, a word like "peace" or "rest." Hold it there. Keep it there. And if it wanders, bring it back again.

Do this not just once, but every night. And in time, you will find that your sleep deepens. Your thoughts soften. Your life changes. All because you learned the art of mental control.

That is the quiet power of the mind—harnessed, guided, and set free on purpose.

Igniting the Flame Within: Awakening the Power of Vital Living

If we've spoken before of dismantling fear and learning to calm the chaos of the mind, it is now time to move in the other direction—to lift the spirit, to **awaken**, to **ignite** the vital current that flows within you. Too many of us are moving through life as if wrapped in a fog, drifting through our days without fire, without joy, without a trace of the dynamic energy that is our birthright. We go through the motions—working, speaking, eating, surviving—but we do not **live**. Not truly. Not consciously.

Let me be frank: a great many people are alive only in the biological sense. Their hearts beat, their lungs breathe, but their inner world—the place where energy and purpose reside—is stagnant. They operate on low power, like dim lanterns flickering in the wind. Their steps lack conviction. Their words lack intention. Their eyes, when you meet them, reveal nothing but repetition and fatigue. This is not living. This is existing.

But life, true life, does not exist merely in motion or function. It exists in **vitality**—in the electric sense of aliveness that floods you when you are fully engaged with your own existence, when every cell in your body, every thought in your mind, every beat of your heart feels awake and aligned with purpose.

And so today, I want to challenge you to **claim your energy**, to step into the full magnitude of your own life force, and to become someone who no longer merely endures the day, but who inhabits it with power and presence.

You were not born to be a machine. You were not placed here to grind through routines, ticking off hours and tasks like some weary cog in the clockwork of society. You were made to feel the pulse of life running through your veins. You were made to create, to feel, to act with intention, to change things, to move the world around you by the sheer force of your being. But none of this can happen unless you awaken the vital spark within.

Let us begin, then, with this truth: **Life is movement**. Life is flow. When energy is stagnant, it begins to decay. When a river stops flowing, it becomes a swamp. So, too, with the human spirit. The moment you stop caring, stop engaging, stop pushing toward something meaningful, you begin to regress. You begin to rot—not physically perhaps, but emotionally, mentally, spiritually. And eventually, that invisible decay manifests outwardly as lethargy, discontent, apathy, and even disease.

The answer to this is not simply "more effort" or "working harder." That is the mistaken conclusion of the over-industrialized mind. The true solution is found in **rekindling desire**, **reclaiming passion**, and reestablishing a connection to the **life force within you**. You don't need more hours in the day—you need more **life** in your hours.

It is time to inject **vitality** into your speech, your work, your routines, your relationships. When you speak to someone, let your eyes light up. When you begin a task, take a deep breath and start it with full awareness, full presence. When you walk down the street, feel your feet touching the earth with purpose. Stop drifting. Begin **showing up** for your life with enthusiasm.

But how do we begin this process?

It starts by realizing that **vitality is a choice**. Just as thoughts can be guided by the will, so too can your energy be directed by intention. And one of the most powerful tools at your disposal is **affirmation**—not the shallow repetition of empty phrases, but the firm, soul-rooted declaration of truth that rewires your inner state. You must speak life into your body. You must call it awake.

Let your new mantra be this:

"I am alive."

Not just in form, but in spirit. Say it with conviction. Say it every morning as you rise. Say it as you brush your teeth, as you pour your coffee, as you walk into your office or sit at your desk. Whisper it under your breath when you feel tired. Shout it in your mind when you feel defeated. Let it become your battle cry against inertia. **"I am alive."**

And as you say it, **see it**. Picture your body brimming with energy, your lungs expanding with purpose, your heart pumping courage through your veins. See yourself filled with a golden current of power, strength, optimism, drive. Let your thoughts align with this vision and act accordingly.

When you begin a new task, tell yourself: **"I bring life to this."** Whether it's cleaning your kitchen, writing an email, building a business, or creating a piece of art—whatever you do, **pour your life force into it**. That is how the ordinary becomes extraordinary. That is how work becomes joy. It is not what you do that gives your life meaning—it is how much life you bring to what you do.

Apathy is the enemy of greatness. Lethargy is the thief of joy. Do not let them seduce you with comfort and routine. Stand up, even if you feel weary. Take a cold shower. Go for a walk. Breathe deeply and with purpose. Shake off the dust from your soul and return to your core. There is **fire in you still**, and it waits only for you to strike the match.

To help you anchor this awakening, practice the following affirmation exercise each day:

Daily Vitality Activation Exercise

1. **Stand upright**, feet planted firmly, spine straight, shoulders back.
2. Take a **deep breath**, slow and full. As you inhale, say in your mind:
3. "I am breathing in life."
4. Hold that breath for a few seconds and **visualize energy flooding your body**.
5. Exhale slowly, and as you do, say:
6. "I release all dullness, all fatigue, all limitation."
7. Repeat this breathing cycle **five times**, each time with growing intensity and belief.
8. Then place your hand on your chest and say aloud:
9. "I AM ALIVE."

    Say it like you mean it. Say it until your whole body vibrates with it.

Repeat this process throughout your day, especially when you feel yourself slipping into autopilot or emotional exhaustion. It will not take long before you feel a real, physical difference.

Remember: you are not a lifeless object drifting through the tide of life. You are **a force**, and like any force, you must be directed, fueled, and focused. Do not squander your days in low-power mode. Do not let the flame dim without ever burning bright.

Get curious. Get hungry. Take an interest in the world around you again. Read something new. Learn a skill. Talk to someone you've never spoken to before. Listen to music that moves you. Touch, taste, notice—engage. The world is still full of wonder, but it will not reveal itself to those who sleepwalk through it.

True energy is not just a matter of good food or rest. It is born from **purpose**. When you know why you are here—when you remember what excites your soul—you will feel energy return to you like a rushing tide. So take time to ask yourself:

What makes me feel alive? What would I do if I felt completely free and limitless?

Then go do a piece of that every day, even in a small way. Even five minutes of doing something that stirs your soul is enough to shift your entire vibration.

And never forget this:

Energy is contagious. The more life you radiate, the more life you attract. The world responds to your state of being. So when you carry yourself with vitality, passion, and fire, you draw opportunities, people, and experiences that match that energy. You become a magnet for movement, growth, joy. You become... **alive**, not just in body, but in essence.

Let this be the beginning of a new chapter. Not just in this book, but in your life.
Let this be the day you **refuse to live halfway**.
Let this be the day you stop existing and start **burning with purpose**.

You are not here to crawl. You are here to **run, dance, shout, create, shine**.

So rise.
And remember:

You are alive.

You are alive.

You are alive.

And that changes everything.

Chapter 10 - Reprogramming the Mind: Mastering Habits for Lifelong Power

There's an invisible power shaping your every decision, your daily routines, and ultimately your destiny. That power isn't willpower. It isn't intellect. It's something far more subtle—habit. More specifically, it's what we'll call the habit-mind, that quiet, automatic force within your subconscious that runs the majority of your life without asking for permission.

You get up each morning and brush your teeth without thinking. You reach for the same breakfast. You speak the same words to your family or coworkers. You think the same thoughts about yourself. And you do these things not because you *decided* to, but because they've been etched into your mental circuitry through the repetition of days, months, or even years.

The truth is this: you are the product of your habits. Not your dreams, not your intentions, not even your goals. All the power in the world means nothing if you can't direct it habitually toward your growth. And all the talent in the world will betray you if your habits move against you.

The great psychologist William James once said, "The great thing in all education is to make our nervous system our ally instead of our enemy." His insight is still as relevant today as it was a century ago, perhaps even more so. If we are to become the architects of our own destiny, we must learn the art of habitual mastery—of deliberately programming our subconscious to work *for* us instead of *against* us.

The Habit-Mind: Your Hidden Ally or Silent Saboteur

Let us begin by understanding what this "habit-mind" actually is. Beneath the surface of your conscious awareness lies a vast, automatic system—the subconscious. This part of your mind does not argue. It does not question. It accepts and obeys whatever you repeatedly feed it. Whether those inputs are empowering or destructive is irrelevant to it. It simply learns through repetition and emotion.

Do something enough times, and it becomes a habit. Think a certain way every day, and it becomes your identity. React with anger or anxiety in enough situations, and soon it becomes your automatic emotional response. This is why the subconscious is so powerful—it quietly molds your behavior without needing your permission.

But herein lies the great opportunity: if we are the ones who built these patterns, then we also hold the power to rebuild them.

The Science of Repetition: Why Habits Stick

Every action you take reinforces a neural pathway. The more often you travel that path, the easier it becomes to follow again. Neuroscientists call this neuroplasticity, the brain's ability to reshape itself based on repeated behavior. Think of it like walking through a field of tall grass. The first time you make your way through, it's difficult. But the more you walk the same path, the more the grass flattens, and the easier the journey becomes.

Now imagine your brain as that field. Every time you choose a behavior—whether it's hitting snooze, checking your phone, reacting with stress, or reaching for a healthy meal—you are literally carving a groove into the landscape of your mind. Those grooves become your defaults. And your defaults become your life.

This is why small, seemingly insignificant actions matter. Every habit is a vote for the kind of person you are becoming. Each repetition is a silent affirmation, a whisper into your subconscious saying: *this is who I am*.

The "Never Skip" Rule: Defending the New Habit

When forming a new habit or breaking an old one, the initial phase is the most delicate. It's during these first days and weeks that your old programming fights hardest to survive. This is when the temptation to say *"just this once"* arises—a voice that seems innocent, but is, in truth, the first crack in your armor.

You must treat these moments as sacred. Every time you resist the old pattern and act in alignment with the new one, you strengthen the neural pathway of your desired habit. Each repetition is like pouring concrete into the foundation of a new structure. Skip too many days in a row, and you delay the formation of the habit—or worse, begin reinforcing the wrong one.

William James emphasized this very idea when he wrote, "Never suffer an exception to occur until the new habit is securely rooted in your life." Consider this the golden rule of transformation. Every time you follow through, the habit becomes easier. Every time you break it, the habit becomes weaker.

Habits Are Emotional

One of the overlooked elements of habit formation is emotion. It's not enough to simply repeat a behavior like a robot. If you want it to stick, you must *feel* something as you do it.

Attach a sense of pride to your new habit. Celebrate each small win. Visualize the person you are becoming. Connect your action to your larger vision. This emotional reinforcement speeds up the programming process and tells your subconscious: *This matters. Keep doing it.*

When you treat every healthy meal, workout, focused work session, or act of kindness as a sacred act of self-alignment, you embed it more deeply into your identity. You are not just repeating a behavior—you are becoming a new version of yourself.

The Folding Paper Analogy: How Patterns Deepen

Let me offer you a metaphor.

Imagine your mind as a sheet of paper. Every time you fold that paper in a certain direction—every time you think a thought or take an action—it creates a crease. The more you fold along that same line, the deeper the crease becomes. Eventually, the paper almost folds itself.

This is exactly what happens with your thoughts, emotions, and behaviors. If you've folded your mind into anxiety, procrastination, or self-doubt thousands of times, those patterns are deep. But you can still make new folds. With intention and persistence, you can train your mind to bend in a new direction. It will be stiff at first, awkward, resistant. But with repetition and focus, that new fold becomes your new default.

Practical Steps to Habit Transformation

Let us now lay out a clear path to reprogramming the habit-mind. These steps may seem simple—but do not mistake their simplicity for lack of power.

1. Decide Who You Want to Become

Before any habit becomes powerful, it must connect to an identity. You must clearly decide: *Who am I becoming?* The more vivid and compelling your vision of yourself, the more fuel your subconscious has to work with.

"I am a focused creator."
 "I am a calm and grounded person."

"I am someone who always follows through."

Anchor your habits to these identities.

2. Start Small, Repeat Often

Big change happens through small, consistent action. Instead of trying to revolutionize your life overnight, commit to one or two powerful habits and repeat them daily. If you want to be a writer, write one sentence each morning. If you want to be calm, take one deep breath before every conversation.

Consistency beats intensity.
Repetition creates reality.

3. Use Triggers and Anchors

Habits stick better when they are tied to existing routines. Choose a current habit and attach your new habit to it.

Example:
"After I brush my teeth, I say my affirmation."
"After I pour my coffee, I visualize my goals."

These anchors help create predictable cues for your subconscious.

4. Visualize and Feel the Habit

Each time you engage in your habit, pause to visualize the future version of yourself it's building. Feel the pride, the momentum, the expansion. Let your body and nervous system absorb the emotion of progress.

5. Track and Celebrate Progress

What gets measured, improves. Use a simple habit tracker. Mark each day you follow through. Keep the streak alive. And celebrate—even small milestones. Let your brain associate habits with success, joy, and forward motion.

6. Guard Against the "Exception" Voice

The most dangerous phrase in habit-building is:

"Just this once."

Each time you hear it, respond with:

"Not today. I am not that person anymore."

This strengthens your resolve and reinforces your new identity.

Becoming the Master of Your Habit-Mind

There will be days when you falter. Days when old habits whisper your name. Days when change feels too slow. On those days, return to this truth: you are not your past. You are what you repeatedly do from this moment forward.

The habit-mind is a neutral machine. It will drive you toward discipline or destruction depending on your programming. Your job is to seize the steering wheel—to be the conscious programmer of your patterns. The future belongs not to those with perfect talent, but to those who build automatic excellence.

So fold the paper in a new direction.
 Repeat the action.
 Repeat the identity.
 And soon, the transformation will no longer be effort—it will be effortless.

You will have become your habits.

And your habits will have become your power.

Chapter 11

Mastering Emotional Habits: Rewiring the Feelings That Shape Your Life

From *Mind Magnet* by Jonathan W. Hale

When people think of emotions, they often see them as spontaneous, uncontrollable forces—whirlwinds that emerge from within and sweep us into joy, rage, sadness, or envy. We accept emotions as deeply personal and instinctual, often separating them from thought or habit, as though they arise independently of our will. But here lies one of the most overlooked truths in psychology: emotions are habits, too. And like all habits, they can be rewired.

It may sound surprising at first, even contradictory. How can something as raw and instinctual as an emotion be shaped like a behavior? How can you "practice" not feeling jealous or stop yourself from plunging into anger? But modern psychology—and ancient wisdom—agree on this essential truth: repetition deepens emotion, and awareness allows transformation.

Emotions Are Learned Responses

Every emotion you feel is not just a reaction to what's happening outside you. It's also a reflection of what's been conditioned inside you. If you've practiced getting angry every time you're criticized, or worried every time the unknown appears, then those reactions have become default patterns. Your nervous system has memorized them like grooves in a record.

The saying "emotions deepen by repetition" is not just poetic—it's neurological fact. Each time you surrender to an emotion and let it run its course, you make it more likely to return. Just as muscles grow stronger through repeated use, so do emotional reactions. Give jealousy a little room, and it starts rearranging the furniture. Let anger stay the night, and soon it moves in permanently.

The Poison of Passive Emotion

Negative emotions rarely come all at once. They creep in subtly, often disguising themselves as justified concern. Take jealousy, for example. It begins with a twinge, a whisper of suspicion. You dismiss it at first, but then it returns—louder, more convincing. And before you know it, you're spinning stories, mistrusting others, and poisoning your peace of mind. What started as a spark becomes a wildfire.

The same applies to worry. At first, you worry about major events—finances, health, your children. But soon, the habit of worry grows stronger than its subject. You start worrying about delays, glances, and weather forecasts. Worry becomes a lens through which you interpret life itself.

Negative emotional habits are not only harmful to your peace—they're visible to others. Worry etches deep lines in your face, turns your voice brittle, and your presence heavy. Chronic anger erodes your health and relationships. Envy distorts your thinking. And habitual pessimism keeps blessings from being recognized, let alone multiplied.

Emotional Habits and Identity

Here's where it becomes even more important: emotional habits slowly form your identity. Each time you give in to a certain emotional response, your subconscious updates its understanding of "who you are."

You're not just someone who "got angry"—you become someone who *is angry*. Not just someone who "felt anxious"—but someone who *is an anxious person*.

But here's the liberating truth: if you can rehearse a destructive emotion into permanence, you can rehearse its opposite with equal success. You can practice joy. You can repeat gratitude. You can train serenity. And over time, these emotions, too, will deepen into habits, until they feel just as automatic, just as natural, as the negative ones they replaced.

The Psychology of Reversal: Emotional Reprogramming

How do you unlearn a negative emotional habit?

First, recognize that you are not helpless. Emotions may feel automatic, but they are not immune to will. They can be redirected. They can be neutralized. They can be replaced.

Second, catch the emotion early. Don't wait until it has possessed your body, thoughts, and voice. At the first flicker of fear, jealousy, irritation—pause. Breathe. Label it. Acknowledge it. "Ah, there's that old reaction."

Now take action. This is your window. This is where your power lives.

Method One: Command It to Leave

Yes, you read that right. Speak to the emotion as though it were a stubborn house guest.

"Out! You don't belong here."

It may resist. It may linger. But the very act of interrupting its pattern sends a signal to your subconscious: *I am in charge.*

With repetition, this gets easier. The emotion loses its grip. Your will gets stronger. Your brain builds new circuits. What was once automatic becomes obsolete.

Method Two: Replace With the Opposite Emotion

Nature abhors a vacuum. It is not enough to simply push a negative emotion out—you must pull a positive one in.

If you feel jealousy, replace it with admiration. If you feel anger, replace it with understanding. If you feel worry, replace it with trust.

Choose a thought, a memory, or even a person that represents this better emotion. Dwell on it. Speak it aloud. Smile with it. And your mind will begin to associate situations differently.

Method Three: Reprogram the Body

William James, a brilliant pioneer of psychology, wrote:

"Smooth the brow, brighten the eye, contract the dorsal rather than the ventral aspect of the frame... and speak in a major key."

In simpler terms: change your posture, your breath, and your voice—and your emotions will follow.

It may seem artificial at first, but your physiology speaks louder to your subconscious than your thoughts do. Stand tall. Open your chest. Breathe deeply. Lift your voice. These actions tell your mind: *I am not afraid. I am not weak. I am not broken.*

Emotional Hygiene: A Daily Discipline

Just as you brush your teeth each day, clean your emotional state. Take five minutes each morning to rehearse the emotions you want to embody.

Say: "Today, I choose calm. I choose strength. I choose gratitude."

Picture yourself moving through the day with grace. Anticipate moments of challenge and pre-program your reactions. The more often you do this, the more your body and mind will respond automatically.

Beware the Emotional "Just Once"

The single most dangerous phrase in emotional reprogramming is:

"Just this once."

Just this once, I'll indulge the anger. Just this once, I'll let jealousy burn. Just this once, I'll let fear dictate.

Every time you give in, you reopen the door. You reinforce the old circuit. You make it more likely to return.

Instead, hold the line. One moment of discipline protects you from ten moments of recovery.

The Garden of the Heart

Think of your emotional life as a garden. Every thought is a seed. Every emotion is a plant. You choose what to water. You decide what to prune. Let envy, worry, bitterness, or resentment grow, and they will overtake the beauty. But nurture joy, peace, compassion, strength—and soon, they will fill every corner of your being.

You don't have to be perfect. But you must be deliberate.

Final Word: Emotion as Energy

Remember this: emotion is energy in motion. If you don't direct it, it will direct you. You are not powerless. You are the conductor. You hold the baton. You decide the tempo, the volume, the tone.

So take control. Shape your emotional habits with the same care you would give to your thoughts, your body, your finances, or your relationships. Because your emotions—when mastered—become your greatest source of strength, connection, and purpose.

Choose them well. Practice them daily. And let your emotional habits become a reflection of your highest self.

Chapter 12 — Growing a Better Mind: Creating New Patterns of Thought

Throughout the earlier chapters, we've discussed letting go of unhelpful feelings and training the habit-mind. Now, let's go a step further—toward the active cultivation of powerful emotional and mental states by developing entirely new thought patterns. You're not merely trying to suppress fear, hatred, or anxiety—you're awakening dormant brain potential that can anchor a new, better version of yourself.

We begin with a truth that modern psychology is finally catching up to: you are not your emotions. Your feelings and moods are not permanent features of who you are—they are habits, and habits can be changed.

Most people walk through life assuming that their sadness, anxiety, irritability, or lack of motivation is simply "who they are." They say things like, "I've always been like this," or "That's just how I'm wired." And so, without meaning to, they surrender control of their mind to old emotional grooves worn deep by repetition and belief.

But here is the liberating truth: those grooves are not destiny—they're just old patterns. And your brain is capable of growing new ones.

We now understand that the brain is plastic—it can be reshaped, re-trained, and restructured. With effort and repetition, you can stimulate the growth of new neural pathways that support joy, love, optimism, courage, clarity, and purpose.

So how do you do it?

The Strategy of Replacement

As we touched on previously, the most effective way to get rid of a negative mental habit is not to fight it directly. Instead, you introduce a powerful opposing force. You don't overcome darkness by shouting at it—you light a lamp. Similarly, to dissolve hate, you must generate love. To cast out worry, grow confidence. To calm fear, cultivate faith.

This may sound poetic, but it is deeply practical. Every thought, every emotional state you dwell in, strengthens certain connections in the brain. The more often you activate a particular pattern, the more easily it activates in the future. That's how habits are formed—and also how they are broken.

For instance, when you make a consistent effort to focus on compassion, the brain begins building and reinforcing the neural architecture that supports compassionate behavior. This is not speculation—it's a process that can be measured. Scientists have documented changes in brain structure resulting from as little as eight weeks of practicing gratitude or mindfulness.

This principle applies to any state of mind. You must practice the one you want, deliberately and consistently, until it becomes stronger than the one you're trying to replace.

Stop Working Old Cells to Death

Your brain is filled with untapped potential. You have billions of neurons—and most of them lie dormant. The majority of people rely on a very small subset of their mental capacity, repeating the same thought loops over and over until those pathways are worn thin.

Imagine a pianist who only plays five keys on the keyboard. That's how most people use their minds.

But just like the musician who decides to practice new scales and compositions, you can stimulate fresh brain activity by consciously choosing new patterns of thought and action. The first few times, it may feel awkward—just like learning a new instrument—but if you persist, those new pathways grow strong, and the old ones lose power through disuse.

Reframing Negative Identity

Many people define themselves by their emotional patterns. "I'm an anxious person." "I'm not good with people." "I'm lazy." These statements are not facts—they are judgments based on repeated feelings and past actions. And every time you reinforce them, you breathe more life into them.

Instead, replace these labels with conscious affirmations that support the version of yourself you want to grow into:

- "I am becoming more calm and centered each day."
- "I enjoy building connections and speaking clearly."

- "I am discovering my energy and drive."

Then act as if those affirmations are already true. Even if you don't believe them fully yet, behaving in alignment with them stimulates the right areas of the brain—and over time, the belief will follow.

The Mind-Body Feedback Loop

Here's a powerful secret: action and emotion are connected. If you change your body, you change your mood. Sit up straighter. Breathe more deeply. Smile. Move. Take brisk, intentional steps. Look up instead of down. All of this sends signals to your brain that it's time to feel more alive, more present, more capable.

Try it right now. Straighten your spine. Take three deep breaths. Say aloud, with conviction: "I am growing stronger. I am learning to live with joy." Notice the shift that occurs—even if it's subtle.

These small actions plant the seeds of change.

Practical Examples

If you are prone to envy, practice admiration. When you feel that jealous pang, deliberately compliment or celebrate the person's success. This disrupts the old response and begins a new one.

If you struggle with apathy, practice engagement. Set goals, however small. Actively plan your day. Reward effort. Each time you take initiative, you water the seed of motivation.

If fear is your dominant emotion, cultivate bravery—not by doing reckless things, but by taking small, consistent actions outside your comfort zone, and celebrating each one.

The process is not instant—but it is inevitable, if you persist.

Planting the Garden

The mind is a garden. Left untended, weeds grow. You must be the gardener—choose what you want to plant, and water it daily. Starve the weeds. Ignore them. Pull them up when you notice them, but don't let them take your focus.

Water your joy. Fertilize your patience. Tend to your courage, your creativity, your love of learning, your ability to forgive. These are the flowers that will crowd out fear, hate, doubt, and despair.

In time, the mental landscape becomes unrecognizable. The weeds are gone. The soil is fertile. The flowers bloom without strain, because the environment supports them. You've become the person you imagined. Not because you fought to erase the old, but because you grew something better in its place.

You are not a fixed personality. You are not doomed by biology or childhood or even your own mistakes. You are a sculptor with a living block of clay in your hands. That clay is your brain. Shape it wisely.

This chapter has not been a collection of theories—it is a manual for transformation. Start now. Pick one new mental pattern to develop, and act it out today. Repeat it tomorrow. Then again. And again. Until one day, without even trying, it acts itself.

You are not your past patterns. You are the creator of new ones. So create wisely—and create something beautiful.

Chapter 13: The Magnetic Pull of Desire

Desire is not just a passing whim or a fleeting want—it is the engine that drives the universe. Every act of creation, every advancement, every spark of innovation or beauty stems from one root force: the magnetic pull of desire. In this chapter, we explore how desire, when harnessed with intensity and focus, becomes a powerful agent of manifestation.

To begin, imagine desire as a current of energy. Like electricity that powers a machine, desire is the energetic force that animates our goals and breathes life into our dreams. But for this force to have any real effect, it must flow uninterrupted. Fear is the first major obstacle that weakens this current. As we've already discussed, fear acts like static in a radio signal, distorting clarity and reducing the strength of the signal being sent out. Without overcoming fear, desire is weakened at its roots.

Once fear is addressed, we must turn our attention to another invisible threat to our manifesting power: mental leakage. This occurs when our attention is divided, scattered across trivial distractions and shifting desires. In our modern world, saturated with competing demands and constant stimulation, the ability to remain focused on one central aim has become a rare skill—and yet, it is essential. If desire is the current, then attention is the wire that channels it. Frayed or split wires lead to wasted energy. Whole, singular wires carry maximum voltage.

The average person flits from desire to desire—today wanting wealth, tomorrow fame, the next day peace of mind—never giving one wish the full force of their inner power. To truly attract something into your life, you must become intimately connected to it in thought, emotion, and intention. You must fall in love with it—not superficially, but deeply and enduringly.

Think of a young man in love. Everything he does, says, and thinks revolves around the object of his affection. He plans, he dreams, he acts—all in alignment with this central desire. In the same way, when you truly desire something—whether it be a career, a creation, a relationship, or a personal transformation—it must take root in the center of your consciousness. Not in a way that breeds obsession or imbalance, but as a stable, powerful gravitational center that organizes all your smaller thoughts and choices.

Success, in any form, is drawn to individuals who are unwavering in their intent. Desire without focus is a flame that flickers and dies out. Desire with focus becomes a fire that forges reality. This is the magnetic pull of focused intention—when the mind is centered on a single purpose, it becomes a beacon that draws people, opportunities, and circumstances into alignment with the vision.

Mental leaks can take many forms. Sometimes, they appear as self-doubt, envy, or chronic indecision. Other times, they arise as distractions: too many goals, too many voices, too many directions. Each of these drains your internal battery, leaving little energy left for the one thing that truly matters. The key is to identify these leaks and seal them. One method is daily mental inventory—each morning or evening, ask yourself: What am I truly after right now? What has distracted me from it today? What do I choose to refocus on?

When we love something enough, we naturally give it our attention, our effort, and our time. This is why the metaphor of romantic love is so apt. Just as someone in love is consistently pulled toward their beloved, so too are we pulled toward our dominant desires. But just like in love, that relationship requires nurturing. A desire must be fed—not only with thoughts and affirmations but with belief, expectation, and action. If you desire wealth, for instance, but continually reinforce scarcity through your words, habits, and focus, then your desire remains malnourished. Your actions and thoughts must nourish what you wish to grow.

In my own experience, I've seen time and again how simply refocusing on my central aim brought sudden bursts of momentum. Even when no external action was taken—when it seemed I had done all I could and the outcome lay beyond me—just reconnecting emotionally with my goal shifted everything. It's as if the energy I gave to the vision radiated outward, reactivating dormant seeds already planted.

This is the subtle law behind manifestation: attention recharges intention. The act of focusing your emotional energy on your goal acts like sunlight on a plant. Without it, growth is slow or stunted. With it, the internal chemistry of life awakens. The subconscious mind begins to stir, attracting ideas, support, and coincidences that move you forward.

And yet, many sabotage this process by allowing their desires to become diluted. They want too many things at once, or they allow discouragement to convince them that what they seek is impossible. They flirt with success, but are not committed to it. They court one goal, but are secretly yearning for another. This divided energy creates nothing but frustration. Remember, success—like love—demands fidelity.

To maintain strong desire, there must be emotional fuel. You must care deeply, not just intellectually. You must visualize the goal as if it's already accomplished. You must feel the joy, the satisfaction, the excitement of having it now. This emotional resonance intensifies the attractive power of your desire. It creates a magnetic field that draws your goal closer each day.

Some scientists and metaphysicians have even argued that desire is the hidden law behind the very structure of life. They speak of a kind of universal longing embedded in every atom—an urge to move toward what is needed, what is nourishing, what is fulfilling. The plant reaching toward sunlight is an expression of desire. The tides responding to the moon reflect cosmic attraction. In you, desire is the living proof that you are part of this grand flow of creation.

To cultivate this power, begin by defining clearly what you want. Write it down. Reflect on it. Let it become familiar to you, not as a vague wish but as a vivid, living idea. Next, eliminate distractions—mental, emotional, and practical. Reduce your energy leaks. Choose clarity over confusion. Finally, fuel the fire of your desire each day with focused attention, action, and belief. Let your love for the goal grow so strong that no setback can diminish it.

When your desire becomes your dominant mental and emotional note, it acts like a magnet pulling the future into the present. This is not mysticism—it's a law of mental focus and emotional alignment. Every great accomplishment began in the fertile soil of intense desire. When you love what you seek, and commit to it with your full self, the universe cannot help but respond.

So remember: fall in love with your vision. Stay faithful to it. Focus your energy. Nurture your desire. And above all, don't scatter your heart across a dozen fleeting wishes. One true aim, pursued with passion, is more powerful than a hundred half-hearted hopes.

Chapter 14: The Inner Engine of Achievement — Energy and Determination Unleashed

There is a power within every human being—an invisible force that separates those who thrive from those who merely survive, those who move forward from those who remain stagnant. You may have noticed this difference yourself—between the ones who seem to bend life to their will, and the others who drift aimlessly, always reacting but never creating. The difference is not in physical strength, nor in intelligence, wealth, or opportunity, though these things may contribute. The real distinction lies deeper, in the realm of energy and unwavering resolve.

The late philosopher and writer Edward Burton once observed something profound: "The longer I live, the more certain I am that the great difference between men—the feeble and the powerful, the great and the insignificant—is energy and invincible determination. A purpose once fixed—and then death or victory." His words strike a chord, for they capture the essence of personal power in just a few clear strokes. And if you reflect on them deeply, you'll realize they hold the very key to unlocking nearly anything worth striving for in this life.

It is not enough to possess energy alone. You must also know how to direct it. Just as a beam of sunlight is gentle until it is focused through a lens, your energy is only truly effective when it is channeled by the will —by a purpose that consumes you in the most productive and passionate way. There are many people who seem brimming with vitality. They talk fast, move quickly, jump from one project to another with restless urgency. But observe them closely and you will often find them scattered, lacking the focused discipline to see any single goal through to completion. Their power bleeds into distractions and half-measures, leaving little to show for their potential.

Energy without direction is like a river without banks—spread wide, but shallow. It floods everything, yet nourishes nothing. What transforms this raw potential into a life-changing force is **invincible determination** —the kind of resolve that makes retreat unthinkable, that sets its sights and does not stray until the goal is achieved or death intervenes. This is not drama. This is clarity. The world has always been shaped by those who adopt this mindset. Their talents may vary, their backgrounds may differ, but they share a fierce and relentless will to see something through, no matter the cost.

Now, you might say: "That sounds powerful, but I don't know if I have it in me." And to that, I say: **You do**—just as every human does. Every one of us has within us a giant will, dormant perhaps, but no less real. The problem isn't absence of power, but absence of decision. Most of us float through life without ever summoning that inner giant, content with vague wishes and half-hearted efforts. We don't fully commit. We say "I want," but rarely "I will." And it is only when the latter is spoken—clearly, decisively, with no room for escape—that the sleeping force within us stirs and rises.

If you have never done this before, you might be amazed at what follows. Energy will surge through you. Ideas will become actions. Obstacles that once seemed immovable will begin to shift. That is the power of the will—of invincible determination. It is one of the great dynamic forces of the universe, as potent in its way as gravity or electricity. And yet, unlike those elemental forces, this one lives inside you, waiting for you to claim it.

Consider for a moment the men and women society regards as "great." Writers, thinkers, statesmen, entrepreneurs, inventors. From a distance, we imagine they must be made of different stuff—that they were born gifted or lucky or favored by fate. But if you were to sit beside them, share a meal, hear their unpolished thoughts, you'd find something surprising: they're often remarkably ordinary. They don't shine in every moment. They don't speak like geniuses or act like legends. And yet—they've done what few do. They've found their aim and refused to let go.

What sets them apart is not the glow of their intellect or the beauty of their words, but their ability to channel themselves—consistently, quietly, with force—toward what they want. They've chosen not to scatter their light, but to aim it like a laser. They believe in themselves and behave accordingly. Their success is not made in moments of inspiration but in years of steady application.

Many people fail not because they lack ability, but because they spread themselves too thin—trying to impress, trying to do everything at once, trying to be admired instead of effective. They want to show the world how clever they are before they've actually accomplished anything. In contrast, those who truly achieve tend to be quiet, focused, and uninterested in applause until after the results speak for themselves.

If you spend time around successful individuals, you might begin to absorb their unspoken lessons. You'll notice that they keep their attention tight. They don't waste their brilliance in idle conversations or try to outshine others in casual settings. They conserve their energy like firewood in winter, using it only where it counts. Their habits of concentration, their internal discipline, and their refusal to entertain every passing whim—these are what elevate them above the masses.

And so, if you take one message from this chapter, let it be this: stop undervaluing yourself, and stop imagining that the successful are made of something you lack. You are composed of the same elements, carved from the same substance. You already possess everything required to change your life. But you must **choose**—choose to direct your energy, choose to believe in your own ability, and choose to resist the constant lure of distraction.

Energy and determination, when bound together by will, become a force that can shatter limitations. They allow you to begin again where others stop. They drive you when motivation fades. They make progress inevitable.

Let these words burn themselves into your being:

"Energy and Invincible Determination."

Say them aloud. Repeat them in moments of doubt. Let them become a part of your mental bloodstream. They are not just words—they are the very fuel of achievement.

The time has come for you to stop doubting your power and start directing it. Decide what matters. Pour yourself into it. Ignore the crowd. Focus your efforts. And remember: **the world does not reward noise—it rewards results.**

CHAPTER 15 OWN WHAT'S ALREADY YOURS

There's a strange habit many of us fall into—one that quietly robs us of the joy, progress, and fulfillment that could be ours. I remember speaking with a woman not long ago who had, after many years of silent yearning, finally come close to attaining something she deeply desired. The dream she had nursed like a fragile flame seemed, at last, within reach. And yet—what did she say? "Oh, it's too good to be true... it's too good for me." Her words were trembling with disbelief, not because the goal was unreachable, but because she had not yet realized something fundamental: **we cannot receive what we are unwilling to claim**.

That woman stood at the edge of her promised land, yet her heart hesitated at the threshold. Not because the gates were closed, but because she hadn't yet given herself permission to walk through them. Like many others, she had been hypnotized by the illusion that some dreams are reserved for the chosen few. But life is not a lottery. The universe does not operate on favoritism. It operates on alignment—and alignment begins when we believe we are worthy of what we desire.

Let me say it plainly: **Nothing is too good for you.** Absolutely nothing.

It doesn't matter what you've done in the past, how imperfect your journey has been, or what voices—internal or external—have told you otherwise. The highest, brightest, richest experiences this life has to offer are not the private inheritance of some elite class of humans. They are the rightful inheritance of anyone brave enough to recognize that **desire itself is a signal of possibility.** You would not yearn for a thing you were not meant to reach.

The world is not waiting to give you permission. It is waiting for you to raise your hand.

We've all been taught, in subtle ways, to "be realistic," to keep our expectations low, and to bow our heads in humility when something beautiful enters our life. But that humility, when exaggerated into self-denial, becomes a self-fulfilling prophecy. "I'm not ready," "It's not for me," "I don't deserve this"—these are not just statements. They are **commands to the subconscious** and signals to the laws of attraction that you are not yet prepared to receive.

And the Law listens. Oh, yes—it listens with exactness. It mirrors your deepest assumptions. If you tell it, "I'm not good enough," it nods and rearranges your reality to confirm that belief. If you say, "This dream is too big for me," the Law respectfully steps back and lets the dream drift by. But when you stand tall, breathe deep, and declare, "This is mine," the universe rushes to meet your energy.

What you declare with confidence, you magnetize with power.

This isn't about arrogance. It's not about pretending to be more than you are. It's about remembering **who you truly are.** You are not a bystander in this life. You are not a ghost in your own story. You are the living expression of Infinite Potential—an extension of Source itself—and your very presence on this earth is evidence that the highest gifts of existence are already encoded within you. To reach for what you want is not theft. **It is your birthright in motion.**

And the key to activating that birthright? Desire. Expectation. Courage.

These are not abstract virtues. They are **active forces.** They are tools you must sharpen, wield, and direct with intention. The desire for a better life is not foolish—it is sacred. Expectation is not naïve—it is creative. And courage is not a luxury of the strong—it is the bridge between knowing and becoming.

But remember: before these powers can work for you, they must be anchored in the unshakable belief that what you seek is already yours. Not because you stole it. Not because you tricked the system. But because you finally stopped arguing against your own worth.

There is no spiritual merit in shrinking yourself. There is no divine reward for dimming your light. The so-called "virtue" of false humility has kept too many powerful souls trapped in cages built from their own thoughts. Let me be very clear: **you do not honor the universe by settling for less. You honor it by stepping fully into what it has placed inside you.**

So stand up. Lift your gaze. The treasures of this world—love, joy, abundance, creativity, success—are not locked in a vault. They are strewn at your feet like toys in a cosmic kindergarten. And just like children, you are meant to play. To build. To create. To enjoy. The tools of this life—homes, opportunities, relationships, achievements—are not the destination. They are the sandboxes and building blocks of your becoming.

Don't be shy about asking for them. Don't tiptoe through the world like a guest afraid to open the fridge. This is your house. This is your playground. **Reach for it. Demand it. Use it.** Not to inflate your ego, but to expand your soul.

And when you've finished playing with one toy, don't cling to it. Let it go. There are more waiting. The Master of Life understands this: that the things of the world are **tools**, not trophies. Use them, but don't worship them. Enjoy them, but don't depend on them. Own them, but never let them own you.

This is where the truly powerful separate from the merely ambitious. The Slave of Circumstance believes that life is something that happens to him. He worships the few good things he stumbles across and fears they'll be taken away. He sees toys as treasures and clutches them with white knuckles, never realizing that there's an entire storehouse waiting for him if only he'd ask.

But the Master of Circumstance? She walks differently. He speaks differently. She knows the supply is endless. He knows his right to it. She asks. He receives. She plays. He grows. And when it's time to move on—to let go of what once served her—she does so with grace, knowing the next gift is already on its way.

Be that Master. Be that Child of Power.

The world may call it arrogance. Let them. The truth is, **it's alignment.**

You were not born to beg. You were not born to shrink. You were not born to apologize for your brilliance.

You were born to claim what's already yours.

So ask boldly. Expect richly. Walk confidently.

The Law is listening. What will you dare to ask for today?

CHAPTER 16 THE LAW IS ALWAYS WORKING

Not long ago, I found myself deep in conversation with a man who was adamant—almost proudly so—that the concept of "attracting" things with thought was utter nonsense. "It's all luck," he declared, folding his arms with conviction. "Some people are born lucky. Others, like me, have nothing but bad luck chasing them their whole lives." He went on to explain how everything he touched fell apart, how every opportunity turned into a disaster, and how he had come to expect failure as naturally as the sunrise.

As he spoke, I couldn't help but marvel—not at the content of his words, but at the invisible power they carried. You see, without realizing it, he was providing the most powerful confirmation of the Law of Attraction I could have asked for. His entire life was a living demonstration of the principle, though he remained blind to the engine running beneath it.

This man believed—deeply, instinctively, and with total certainty—that things would go wrong. And they did. Not because the universe was cruel. Not because fate had singled him out for suffering. But because his **expectation** was the mold into which his reality was poured. He had built his own prison with bricks made of belief.

It is a profound truth: **the Law of Attraction is not activated only when you consciously "wish hard enough."** It is always in operation, like gravity, whether you acknowledge it or not. It doesn't wait for your approval. It responds, instead, to your dominant state of mind. And your **deepest beliefs**—those quiet, often unspoken convictions—carry far more power than any half-hearted desire or fleeting affirmation.

There are those who believe success requires dramatic effort, desperate prayer, or mystical rituals. But often, success comes more quietly: to the one who walks forward with steady conviction that **it will all work out.** Not hope. Not vague optimism. But quiet certainty. He may stumble. He may fail. He may even fall flat on his face. But inside, the fire never wavers. He knows he's moving toward something real.

That knowing draws opportunities like iron to a magnet.

And what of the man who expects failure? What else could he attract? Every action, every decision, every mood is colored by that belief. He becomes tense when ease is needed, hesitant when boldness is called for, and defeated before the race begins. His subconscious, loyal and obedient, helps sabotage every plan—because it believes that's what he wants. Because that's what he's always believed.

You see, belief **is** the engine behind the law. And expectation is the fuel.

This isn't magic. It's not mysticism. It's **mental alignment**. When your inner world broadcasts certainty—whether in the direction of joy or misery—your outer world adjusts to match it. This is the real science behind success and failure, behind victory and collapse. **It is law, not chance.**

People love to blame "bad luck." But luck is only the name we give to **unseen law.**

There is no such thing as chance in the grand machinery of life. Behind every apparent coincidence is a chain of causes, stretching far back into the hidden depths of thought, emotion, and intention. You may not see those causes clearly. You may not remember the thoughts you sent out, or the feelings you entertained. But they were there—and they did their work.

Like a seed planted in the dark, your dominant belief always blossoms into experience.

When a stone tumbles down a mountainside, we may call it chance. But in truth, countless subtle forces—gravity, wind, erosion, vibration—worked for years to bring it to that point. The same is true in your life. No experience is random. No event is untethered from cause. Whether it's a victory or a struggle, a triumph or a heartbreak—it is the fruit of your inner climate.

And here's the empowering truth: **you can change that climate.**

If you are tired of being tossed around by unseen forces—if life feels like a storm that won't end—then it is time to stop drifting and start aligning. Because you are never outside of the law. You are either **working with it or against it**. There is no neutral ground.

The Law does not care whether you understand it. But your life will.

You can either be the confused object being pushed around by its power, or you can be the conscious architect who learns to shape his world with it. You can wrestle against the current, blaming the river, or you can build a boat and sail.

The Law of Attraction—like all great laws—is impartial. It does not punish. It does not reward. It reflects. It obeys your dominant state. And your thoughts, your moods, your beliefs are all **requests** you send into the universe.

So, what are you requesting today?

You may not shout your beliefs from the rooftops, but they're still echoing through your reality. Are you quietly repeating: "I'm not good enough… I always fail… nothing ever works out for me…"? Or are you affirming, through action and intention: "I belong here… this is possible for me… life is rising to meet me"?

Your life listens not to your words, but to your vibration.

If you want a different result, you must change the note you're singing.

So many people are drowning in negativity, unaware that they're radiating failure long before the facts appear. They wonder why no one trusts them with opportunities. They don't see that **confidence is contagious**, and so is despair. Others pick up your signal. They feel your energy. They respond accordingly.

On the other hand, think of someone who radiates success. You know the type: even when they fall, you say, "Oh, they'll be fine. They always land on their feet." Why do we say this? Because we sense their **inner magnetism.** Their thoughts, beliefs, and actions are synchronized in one powerful frequency. They're in harmony with the law—and the law delivers.

Want to join them?

Then begin here: **change your mental atmosphere.**

Clear the fog of doubt. Sweep away the dust of despair. Let in the light of confidence, courage, and clarity. Set your internal compass to success—not the anxious kind that tries to prove something to the world, but the calm, rooted kind that simply knows. Set your frequency. Send out thoughts of strength. Surround yourself with people who are on the same path. Tune in to the current of success that is flowing all around you. Plug in.

There are thousands—millions—of minds radiating creative, powerful thought every single moment. Why not join the network? Why not tap into that stream of possibility and let it nourish your own vision? The best energy in the world is already in the air. Don't settle for less. Don't disconnect. Align yourself and rise.

The Law is always working. That's the final word.

You can no longer blame chance, nor should you want to. You are too powerful for that. The moment you understand this truth is the moment you stop reacting and start creating. You are not a victim of randomness. You are a channel for intention.

So breathe deeply.

Stand tall.

Think clearly.

And remember…

It is Law. Not chance. Always.

www.ingramcontent.com/pod-product-compliance
Lightning Source LLC
Chambersburg PA
CBHW051423070526
44584CB00023B/3550